A desert is a big stretch gets very little rain. Deserts can be made up of sand or of stones or rock. The Sahara Desert in North Africa is the biggest desert of all.

In some deserts, the sand gets piled up into mounds by the wind. These mounds, which look like waves, are called dunes.

Sometimes, strong winds whip the sand and dust up into sandstorms. When this happens, clouds of sand drift across the desert.

sandstorm

There are tribes who live in the desert. They use camels to ride on and to help them carry things. That is why camels are sometimes called the ships of the desert.

A camel stores fat in its hump. It can go without food or drink for a long time, while it uses up the store of fat. A camel can close its nostrils, which stops sand from getting up its nose in sandstorms.

Deserts often look empty, but lots of animals do live there. There is not much shade or shelter from the sun, so animals hide and do not come out until it is cooler.

Small animals, reptiles, and insects shelter underground from the sun. Desert insects tend to have long legs which help them avoid touching the hot ground.

This insect is from the Namib Desert in South Africa. It drinks while standing on its head by kneeling down and letting droplets from the morning fog drip down its body and into its mouth.

This is a desert fox, called a fennec fox. It lives in the Sahara desert and hunts small animals and insects.

fennec fox

Roadrunners like this one live in deserts in America. They mainly get about by running along the ground, and they feed on insects, lizards, and small snakes.

Deserts often go without rain for a very long time, but sometimes there are sudden rainstorms. When rain falls, the empty riverbeds fill up, and animals can come and drink.

When it has rained, the desert blooms, but only for a short time. Then the seeds lie waiting on the desert sands until the next rainstorm, when they can bloom again.

The cactus has adapted well to life in the desert. When rain falls and the soil is wet, the roots of the cactus take in as much rain as they can. The cactus swells up as it stores the liquid and then shrinks again, little by little, as it uses it up.

Lots of small animals and insects live on the cactus. Desert woodpeckers make holes for nests at the top.

Spadefoot toads live in deserts in America. They can spend a long time underground, waiting for rain. Then they come out into the pools of rain.

The tadpoles of the spadefoot toad only take three weeks to develop into adult toads. By this time, the pools have all dried up, so the toads go back underground to wait for it to rain again.